MINISTRY OF MUNITIONS.

Technical Department- ircraft Production.

I.C. 652.

Kingsway,

W.C. 2.

REPORT

ON THE

HALBERSTADT FIGHTER

TYPE C.L. IV.

OCTOBER, 1918.

I.C. 642.

KINGSWAY,

W.C.2.

REPORT ON THE

HALBERSTADT FIGHTER.

SEPTEMBER, 1918.

The Naval & Military Press Ltd

Published by
The Naval & Military Press Ltd
5 Riverside, Brambleside, Bellbrook
Industrial Estate, Uckfield, East Sussex,
TN22 1QQ England

Tel: +44 (0) 1825 749494
Fax: +44 (0) 1825 765701

www.naval-military-press.com
www.military-genealogy.com

MINISTRY OF MUNITIONS.

Technical Department—Aircraft Production.

▽▽
▽

I.C. 642.

KINGSWAY,
W.C.2.

HALBERSTADT.

REPORT ON THE

HALBERSTADT FIGHTER.

SEPTEMBER, 1918.

J. G. WEIR,
Brig.-General,
Controller, Technical Dept.

T.5.   D.1025/5991.   19/9/18.

REPORT

ON THE

HALBERSTADT FIGHTER.

This machine is a two-seater fighter. It was brought down at Villers Bocage, by Lieutenants Armstrong and Mert on an R.E.8 on 9/6/18. The machine is marked " Type H.S. C.L.2," and bears the military number C.L.2, 15,342/17. The date of construction, 14/4/18, is stamped on various parts. On the side of the fuselage is the following inscription : —

> Leergewicht (weight unladen), 796 k.g.
>
> Nochstbelastung (useful weight), 370 k.g.
>
> Einschl Vollen Tank.   (Including full tanks.)

There is also a red line about 30 inches long drawn at both sides of the fuselage, showing the horizontal in the normal flying position.

GENERAL DETAILS.

The Halberstadt represents, in all probability, the high water mark of two-seater German aeroplane construction, as it is not only well and strongly constructed, but its general behaviour in the air is good according to modern fighting standards.

Its general design will be gathered from the drawings at the end of this report and also from the photographs. Constructional details are dealt with by sketches.

Span of upper plane	35' 3¼"
Span of lower plane	34' 11"
Chord of upper plane	5' 3¼"
Chord of lower plane	4' 3½"
Gap, maximum	4' 0"
Gap, minimum	3' 8½"
Dihedral angle of lower plane	2°
Horizontal dihedral of main planes ...	4°
Total area of main planes	310 sq. ft.
Area of each aileron	11.6 sq. ft.
Area of aileron balance	2.0 sq. ft.
Load per square foot	8.2 lbs.
Area of tail planes	13.6 sq. ft.
Area of elevator	12.4 sq. ft.
Area of fin	6.4 sq. ft.
Area of rudder	7.9 sq. ft.
Area of rudder balance	1.0 sq. ft.
Maximum cross section of body	8.8 sq. ft.
Horizontal area of body	44.0 sq. ft.
Vertical area of body	52.8 sq. ft.
Length over all	24' 0"
Engine	180 H.P. Mercedes
Weight per H.P. (180)	14.07 lbs.
Capacity of petrol tanks	34 gallons
Capacity of oil tanks	4 gallons
Crew	Two
Guns	1 fixed and 1 movable
Military load on test	545 lbs.
Total load on test	2532 lbs.

Speed at 10,000 ft., 97 m.p.h., 1,385 r.p.m.

	Mins.	Secs.	Rate of Climb in Ft./Min.	Indicated Air Speed
Climb to 5000 ft.	9	25	440	69
Climb to 10000 ft.	24	30	240	64
Climb to 14000 ft.	51	55	80	58

Service ceiling (height at which climb is 100 feet per minute), 13,500 feet.
Estimated absolute ceiling, 16,000 feet.
Greatest height reached, 14,800 feet in 64 minutes 40 seconds.
Rate of climb at this height, 50 feet per minute.

STABILITY AND CONTROLLABILITY.

This machine cannot be considered stable. There is a tendency to stall with the engine on, and to dive with the engine off. Directionally, owing to the propeller swirl, the machine swings to the left, but with the engine off is neutral.

Pilots report the machine light and comfortable to fly. The manœuvrability is good, and this feature, taken in conjunction with the exceptionally fine view of the pilot and observer and the field of fire of the latter, makes the machine one to be reckoned with as a " two-seater fighter," although the climb and speed performances are poor judged by contemporary British standards.

PRINCIPAL POINTS OF THE DESIGN.

Single bay arrangements of wings.
Conspicuous set back of the main planes.
Empennage free from wires.
Fuselage tapers to a horizontal line at the rear in direct contra-distinction to the usual German practice.
Pilot's and observer's cock-pit constructed as one.

CONSTRUCTION.

WINGS.

The upper wings are supported by a large centre section having a span of 6 ft. 3 in. This centre section is at right angles to the centre line of machine, but at each side of it; the wings are thrown back with a horizontal dihedral of 4 degrees. The lower wings are smaller in chord and very slightly smaller in span than the upper, and are fixed direct to the lower surface of the fuselage, and it is to be noted that where the trailing edge joins on to the fuselage it is shaped so as to avoid a surface of disconuity at the root of the wing. This is done by smoothly turning upwards the trailing edge.

The actual construction of the wings is of considerable interest, especially on account of the novel type of spar which is employed. This applies to both the upper and the lower planes. The front spar measures $2\frac{3}{4}$ inches by 1 inch and at the butt is placed about 4 inches from the leading edge. It is of " I " section, but is left full at such points as those at which internal bracing wires are fixed. A section of this spar, given in Fig. 1, shows how it is connected to the leading edge by means of ply-wood, both top and bottom.

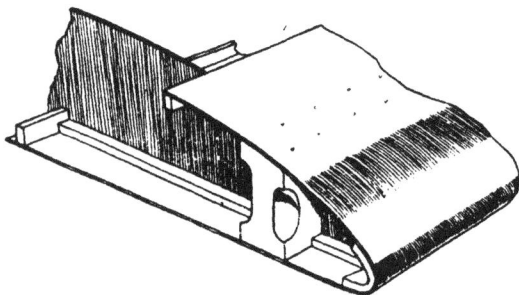

FIG. 1.

FIG. 2.

It will be seen that on the upper surface the ply-wood is extended rearwards for a distance of some $4\frac{3}{4}$ inches from the centre of the spar, and terminates in a small transverse flange about $\frac{1}{2}$-inch deep. This construction furnishes a leading edge of great rigidity and strength, and at the same time it would also appear to be light in weight.

A section of the rear main spar is given in Fig. 2. In this case the main member is of " O " or box section, and is built up of two pieces let into one another in a rather unusual manner. This is clearly shown in the drawing. Both at the top and bottom of the spar, thin strips of wood are used to cover the glued joint, and on this is tacked, both above and below, a flat length of ply-wood 7 inches wide which overhangs the main member of the spar an equal distance at each side.

This ply-wood web is flanged at each end with strips of wood glued in position, and on these strips are fitted small corner pieces which serve to support the ribs. The latter are also of ply-wood, to which are glued and tacked rails of solid wood, top and bottom.

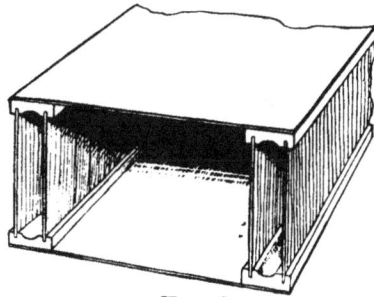

FIG. 3.

A notable point of the wing construction is the fact that steel tubes are not used as the compression members of the internal bracing, as is the common practice. These members are made of box form ribs which occur at intervals along the spars. Adjacent to the root of the wing a very large reinforced box rib occurs, of which the section is given in Fig. 3.

The absence of steel tubes considerably simplifies the attachment of the bracing lugs to the spars, a specimen of which is shown in Fig. 4. It will be noticed that it is of a very simple form, and in this respect it is characteristic of the design of the aeroplane on the whole, which, from this point of view, is far less elaborate than the majority of German designs and appears to be in many ways more practical, especially having regard to quantity production.

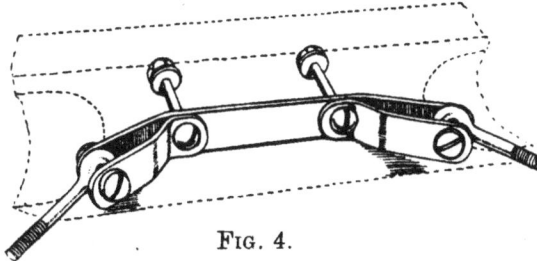

FIG. 4.

WING ATTACHMENTS.

The whole of the centre section, both upper and lower surface, is covered with three-ply wood and the spars used in it are of similar design to those fitted to the wings, and already described. Both the upper and lower wings are provided with attachments which allow of their being very readily taken down. Views of these fittings are given in Figures 5 and 6, the former showing the attachment of the upper wing to the centre section, and the latter that of the lower wing to the

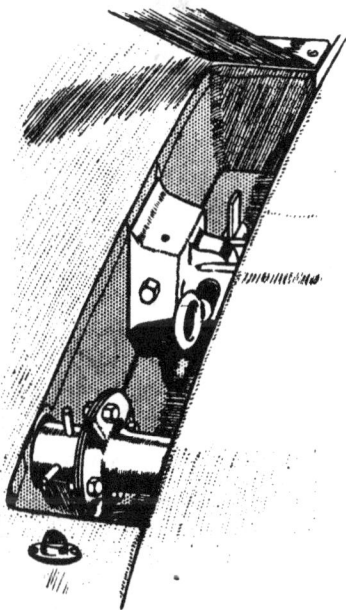

FIG. 5.

FIG. 6.

fuselage. In the former case, the fitting is covered in with a spring operated trap door which also gives access to the joint of the aileron control shaft. A sliding door is used in the lower plane and it will be noticed that the spar is at this point protected by an aluminium foot plate. In each case, quick detachable safety bolts are employed. In Figure 7 are given further details of the type of spar socket in use. This is built up of sheet steel and oxy-acetylene welded, the quality of this work appearing to be very high.

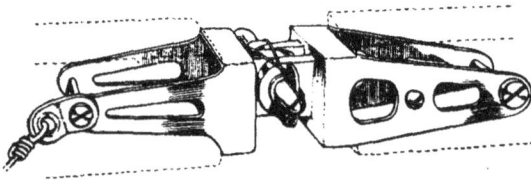

Fig. 7.

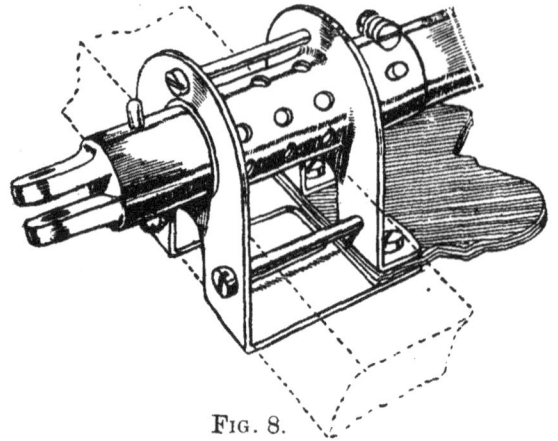

Fig. 8.

The spars of the lower wings engage with a fork-ended tube passing right across the floor of the fuselage, and supported by the longerons of the nacelle by means of the sockets as shown in detail in Figure 8. Here again a high quality of workmanship is evident and it may be said without exaggeration that in this respect the Halberstadt machine is decidedly superior to the other German aeroplanes which have been reported upon, with, perhaps, the single exception of the Fokker.

STRUTS.

The struts throughout this aeroplane are of streamline steel tube of light section, but in contradistinction to the usual German practice they are not tapered at the ends, but end abruptly, as shown in Figure 9. This form of construction has the advantage of lending itself very well to the saving of labour, as the aeroplane struts are simply lengths of plain tubing pierced with transverse holes and reinforced by welded shoulders where the latter occur. The struts are secured top and bottom by bolts and eyes, and it will be noticed that where a cross bracing wire has to be taken from this junction, the turnbuckle is neatly anchored to a small pin passing through the rear of the tubular strut, which is slotted and slightly expanded at this point.

Fig. 9.

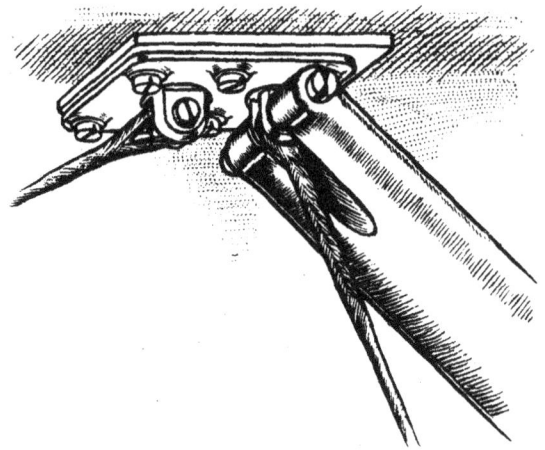

Fig. 10.

The bolt hole is also reinforced by spot welding. This arrangement of strut attachment appears to be very practicable and certainly looks extremely neat.

The upper ends of the inclined centre section struts are fitted with a different type of anchorage, as in this position the simple form of attachment used on the interplane struts cannot be adopted. A sketch is given in Figure 10, from which it will be seen that the end of the strut is welded up solid and fitted with a scooped out slot for the reception of the diagonal wire which runs to the bottom of the fuselage. This wire is very neatly secured by the same bolt as fixes the centre section strut.

The rear spar of the centre section is supported by two vertical struts of the "V" type having their base points attached to the upper members of the fuselage and the apex fixed to the centre section spar. The manner in which the lower joints are fitted to the fuselage brackets and the form of the latter are made clear in Fig. 11.

The bracing wires run as follows:—In the rear between the extremities of the struts; the lift wire in front joins the top of the forward strut to the landing carriage strut. There are no drift wires outside the wings.

FUSELAGE CONSTRUCTION.

One of the most notable points in the Halberstadt fuselage is that whilst it retains the characteristic German form, both forward and amidships, it shows great individuality at the tail, at which point it tapers to a horizontal line, instead of to a vertical line, as is the practice in nearly all

4

other German aeroplanes. The advantage of this arrangement is that the fitting of the tail can be made of sufficient strength without introducing any need for wire bracing. Thus, apart from head resistance, it has less masking effect on the movable gun.

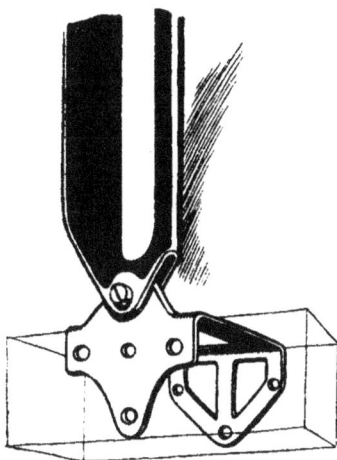

Fig. 11.

The fuselage is constructed in the accepted manner of four main longerons fitted with skeleton bulk heads at intervals and covered in with three-ply wood. The bulk heads are made as shown in Figure 12, and are of a very light construction, except that adjacent to the tail, which serves as the main support of the rudder post and tail plane spar. At this point the bulk head is made of multi-ply wood, and is extensively fretted, as shown in the sketch, Figure 13. Slots are cut for the reception of the longerons. The rudder post is fixed to the bulk head by sheet steel brackets.

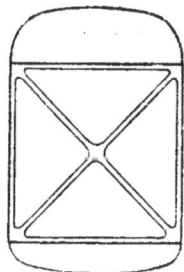

Fig. 12.

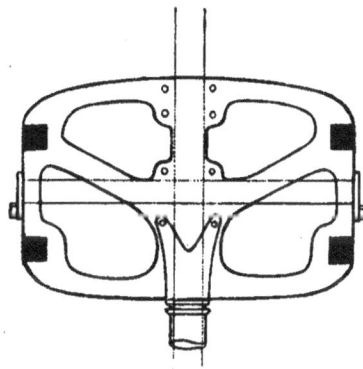

Fig. 13.

The sketch, Figure 14, shows in more detail the fitting of the longerons to this bulk head, and it will be noticed that wedge shaped filling pieces are used, and also that the longeron itself is wrapped with fabric throughout its length. Immediately in front of this tail bulk head, and at each side of the fuselage, a small vertical wooden member is dropped from the upper longeron. This, together with the bulk-head, serves to support the bracket which carries the leading edge of the fixed tail planes. This will be referred to later.

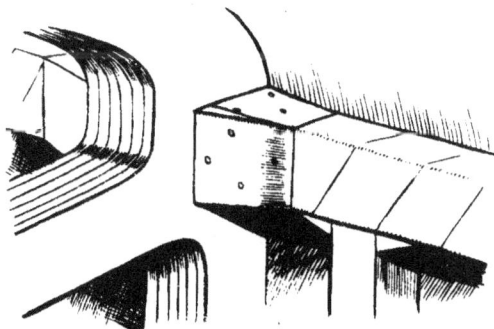

Fig. 14.

Another notable feature of the fuselage is the fact that the pilot's and gunner's cockpits are made in one without apparently introducing any weakness into the construction. This scheme has the advantage of permitting the pilot and passenger to sit very close together, so that the length of the fuselage is reduced. The two cockpits, whilst to all intents and purposes in one, are actually separated by a cross-piece, which is used as a tray for the convenience of the observer. It is, however, probable that the primary object of this crosspiece is to perform a constructional function.

The gun ring does not, as in the usual design, form an integral part of the fuselage coaming, but is fitted thereto by brackets.

FIG. 15.

Inside the observer's cock-pit, the fuselage is reinforced, between the floor and the sides, by slightly curved panels, as shown in the sectional sketch, Figure 15. In the space formed by these panels, run the control wires which are thus out of the way and cannot accidentally be interfered with by the observer.

EMPENNAGE.

As is shown in the general arrangement drawings, the empennage consists of curvilinear fin with balanced rudder, and a semi-circular tail plane to which is hinged a single elevator. As has already been noticed in the description of the fuselage construction, the mounting of these tail planes is carried out without the use of any external wiring or cross bracing. The fixed tail planes are built up of steel tubes, and have a section curved both top and bottom. The rear spar, which acts as part of the hinge of the elevator, is carried in a pair of built-up welded steel brackets, which form the end piece of the fuselage as shown in Figure 16. The front spar, which is slightly in the rear of the leading edge is capable of being adjusted when the machine is on the ground, so as to vary the

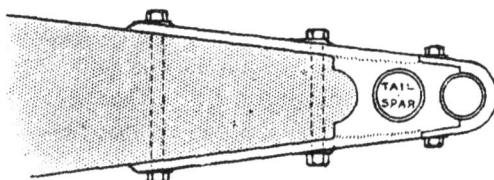

FIG. 16.

angle of incidence of the tail planes. The adjustable clip for this purpose is shown in Figure 17, and gives a choice of four positions. The built-up steel brackets which form this attachment, are carried, one on the rear-most bulk head, shown in Figure 13, and the other on the small vertical strut, noted in Figure 14.

FIG. 17.

6

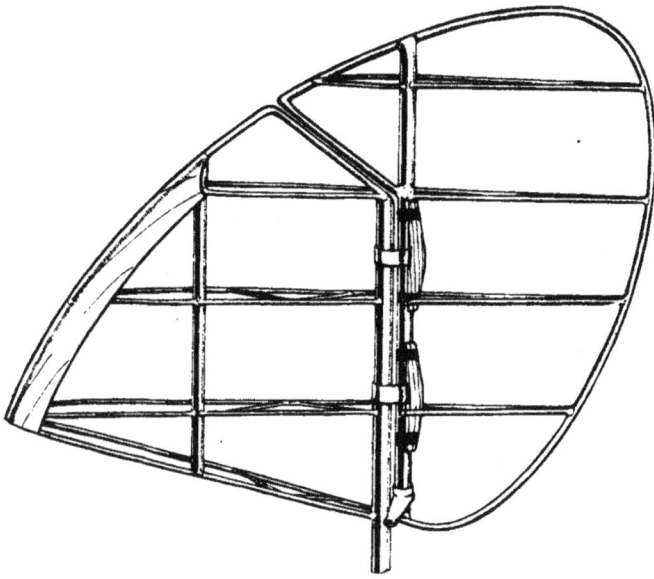

FIG. 18.

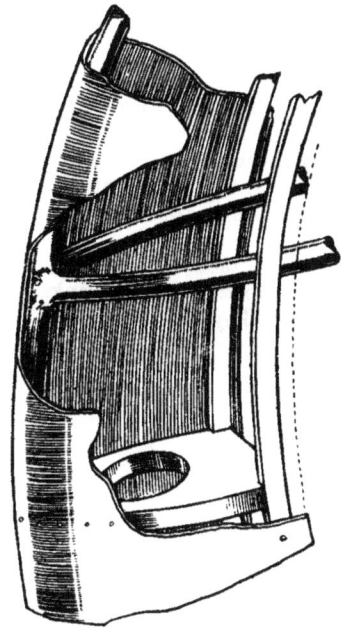

FIG. 19.

The method of construction of the fin and rudder is shown in Figures 18 and 19. The same principle is adopted for the tail planes and elevator. It will be seen that it is a combination of wood and steel construction. The ribs of the fin, which is curved in section, and has a rounded leading edge, consist of thin steel tubes, 8 mms. in diameter welded to the leading spar, and taken back to the rudder post at a slight angle to each other. This staggering of the tubes gives the rib the thickness of a single tube only at the trailing edge. They are reinforced with diagonal tubes of 5 mms. in diameter. The leading edge is formed by a covering of thin three-ply wood supported by a light wooden frame work, the form of which is indicated in Figure 19.

AILERONS.

The ailerons are of the balanced type, and are fitted on the upper plane only. They are furnished with the usual welded steel frame work, and are very light in weight. Their method of operation differs from that found on any other German design. The aileron front spar, which is hinged to the rear spar of the wings, is continued inwards by means of a tubular steel extension until it reaches a point level with the side of the fuselage. Here the extension of the shaft terminates in a crank, which is operated direct by the " T " shaped control lever through the medium of vertical steel rods.

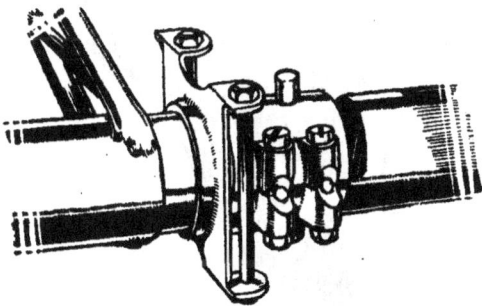

FIG. 20.

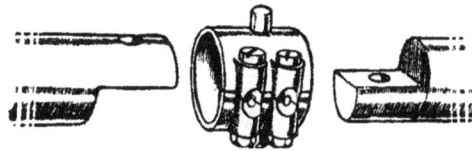

FIG. 21.

The arrangement of these ailerons and their levers may be gathered from the photographs, Nos. A and B. Figure 5 shows how the aileron operating shafts are split and provided with bolted flanges whereby that end of the shaft which is carried in the centre section of the upper plane may be easily detached from the portion which is housed in the wing. Figures 20 and 21 illustrate details of the attachments of the aileron shaft to the aileron itself. The bearings of the shaft consist of a flanged plate at each end, as shown in the drawing, Figure 20. On the inner side is a coupling which unites the front spar of the aileron to the operating shaft. Each of these members terminates in a semi-circular driving dog, and the two are united by a clamped sleeve which is also fitted with a locating cotter pin. This allows the aileron as a whole to be removed very readily in case of need. The tips of the ailerons are turned up at their extremities so as to present, when the controls of the machine are in their normal position, a slightly negative angle to the relative wind. This is in conformity with the usual German practice.

7

CONTROL.

A sketch of the control gear is given in Figure 22. It is, in general, of the usual type, and the lever is fitted with a locking device, whereby the incidence of the elevator can be fixed when desired. This consists of a light telescopic tube arranged diagonally and fitted with a clamp, operated by a thumb screw. The control lever is fitted with an "L" shaped extension at its base, which is pivoted to a long crank bar. This is fitted with bell cranks at each end, and is carried in bearings mounted in the sides of the fuselage in such a manner that the bottom end of the lever is coincident with the centre line of the pivot bearings. As shown in the sketch, the control lever has a "T" piece attached to its foot, which is coupled up through universal links to rods, which extend vertically to the aileron cranks. The ailerons are thus worked entirely positively, and without any cables and pulleys.

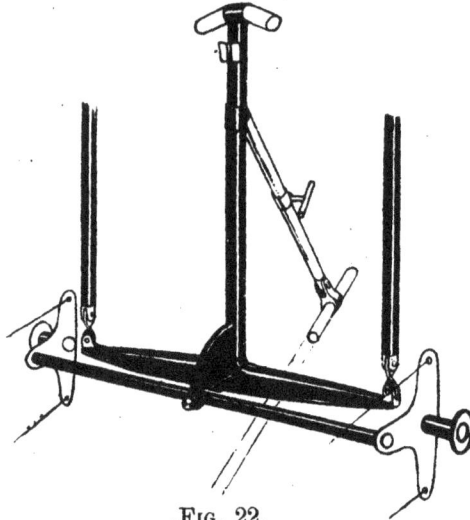

FIG. 22.

Mounted at the head of the control levers, are two triggers for operating the fixed machine guns for which accommodation is provided, though only one was actually found on the aeroplane.

The rudder is controlled by a built up foot bar with the usual heel rests. This is carried in a pivot mounted on a light steel tube fixed across the fuselage longerons. Below this tube the rudder bar pivot carries a grooved pulley of large diameter, over which the rudder wire is passed. It is then taken over pulleys at each side, and down the fuselage to the cranks at the rudder post.

It is worthy of note that whilst none of these controls are duplicated, the elevator cranks are fitted with two sets of bolt holes, so that the leverage can be adjusted if necessary.

FIG. 23.

FIG. 24.

INDERCARRIAGE.

The undercarriage consists of a steel axle, fitted with 760 by 100 wheels. The axle is supported from a pair of tubular steel struts at either side by means of triple steel coil spring shock absorbers. The upper attachment of the undercarriage struts is shown in Figure 23, which illustrates the form of bracket carried on the outside of the fuselage, and bolted to one of the forward bulk heads. The struts are reinforced for the reception of the bolts in a manner similar to that described for the interplane struts.

At their bottom end, the struts are welded together into the form shown in Figure 24, and they are also reinforced by a fixed axle or tie-rod, the sockets of which are slotted for the reception of the turn buckles of the cross-bracing wires.

The undercarriage design is considerably neater than that found on the general run of German aeroplanes, and appears to be both strong and light.

TAIL SKID.

A view of the tail skid is given in Figure 25, and it will be seen that this possesses one or two features of interest.

The skid itself is of ash, reinforced with a light built-up sheet steel shoe. The forward end projects through a hole in the fuselage, and is fitted with the usual shock absorber device which is fastened to the rearmost bulk head.

FIG. 25.

The tail skid is pivoted to an extension of the rudder post, and though it is capable of swinging slightly from side to side, is not actually steerable. Immediately above the shoe of the tail skid, is a second steel shoe, shaped like a spoon, which is rigidly supported by a pyramid of steel tubes The object of this is to prevent any possibility of the elevator cranks coming into contact with the ground, even should the tail strike the earth sufficiently hard to carry the tail skid shock absorber to its limit of extension.

ENGINE.

The engine is a high-compression 160 H.P. Mercedes (commonly known as 180 H.P.), and is of standard type. This engine has been fully described in Handbook No. 805.

ENGINE MOUNTING.

The engine bearers are of wood, and are directly supported by bulk heads in the forward part of the fuselage.

PETROL TANKS.

There are two tanks for petrol. The main supply is carried under the pilot's seat, and has a capacity of 24 gallons. This is fed to the carburetters under air pressure, and the usual hand and engine pumps are employed.

The second tank is let into the upper surface of the centre section of the top plane, and is clearly shown in Photo. B. This contains eight gallons, and is fitted with a glass tube, lying parallel to the upper curvature of the plane, by which the pilot can readily see the level of the fuel. This gravity tank can be filled from the main tank by means of a semi-rotary hand pump.

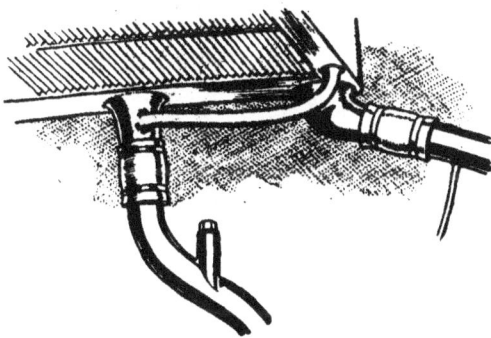

FIG. 26.

FIG. 27.

RADIATOR.

The radiator is of the type which is becoming more and more adopted by German designers, namely, that which is embodied in the upper plane surface. In this case the radiator forms part of the right hand side of the centre section. It is fitted with a small subsidiary water tank, details of which are shown in Figure 27, which is provided with a trumpet nozzle pointing forward. Details of the radiator shutter are given in the photograph No. A. Provision is made for the fitting of a water circulation thermometer, but this instrument was not actually found on the machine. The radiator shutter consists of a sliding panel of sheet steel mounted on a light tubular frame work forming rails. This is within easy reach of the pilot, and can easily be slid forward or backward when it retains its position by reason of the lift effect upon it, and the friction between the guides and the rails.

As shown in sketch, Figure 26, the inlet and outlet pipes of the radiator are both fitted at its left hand front corner, the radiator being furnished with internal baffles, which promote complete circulation of water through all the tubes.   In order to prevent the possibility of an air-lock forming, a small tube is led from the outlet pipe through the bottom of the radiator tank, and is brought close to the bottom side of its top surface.   If air should accumulate in the forward and upper part of the radiator, this tube would quickly allow the lock to be dissipated. ·

The sketch, Figure 26, shows the adapter for the radiator thermometer in the outlet pipe. From the inlet pipe, a small branch is taken off for the carburetter jacket, and from the rear end of the radiator, a pipe provided with a cock, by which the tank can be emptied, is led to the trailing edge of the upper plane.

OIL.

A supply of five gallons of oil is carried in a small tank fitted at the side of the engine.   The latter is furnished with a pump, which, while circulating the lubricating oil contained in the tank. draws a small supply of fresh oil from the tank at every stroke.

PROPELLER.

The screw is of the usual built-up type, and consists of eight laminations of woods in the following order : —

Ash.
Ash.
Mahogany.
Ash.
Mahogany.
Ash.
Mahogany.
Ash.

It has a diameter of 2.4 metres and a pitch of 2 metres and was built at the Luckenwalde Propellerwerke, Niendorf.   In front of the propeller boss proper is a built-up laminated plate to which a spinner is fixed by means of a girdle of stranded steel cable.

WIRELESS.

The aeroplane is internally wired to give greater capacity for wireless and accommodation is provided for the aerial and its spool in the observer's cockpit.   The wireless dynamo, which also provides current for electrically heating clothing, is driven direct from a pulley on the engine, and is mounted on a bracket carried by the left hand engine bearers.

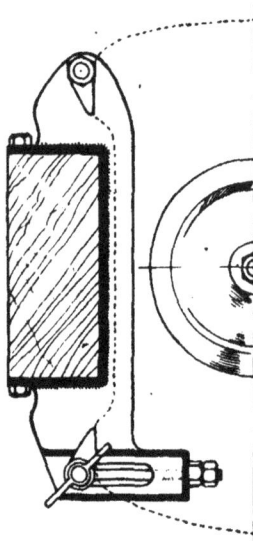

FIG. 28.   FIG. 29.

The form of this bracket is shown in Figure 28, which also indicates the manner in which it is adjustable.   The bracket consists of a flanged and welded sheet steel construction comprising two plates.   The upper extremities of these plates are joined by a transverse bolt on which is hinged a pad against which the foot of the dynamo base is bolted.   A similar bolt and pad is furnished at the bottom of the plates, but in this case the bolt is adapted to slide in a guide so that the tension of the belt can be adjusted and the bolt and its pad locked in any position by a thumb screw.

The dynamo when fitted, lies outside the wall of the fuselage at a point level with the rear of the engine, and is then covered in with a bulbous streamline fairing.   When the dynamo is not (the whole of the wireless apparatus being installed only when actually required) fitted, this streamline fairing, which is readily detachable, has its place taken by a flat panel which can be discerned at the left hand side of the fuselage in photograph No. B.

ENGINE CONTROL.

A throttle lever of the usual ratchet type is fitted at the left hand side of the pilot's cockpit, the carburetter being fitted with an automatic altitude connection. On the dashboard is a screw-down grease pump, for lubricating the water pump spindle.

Ignition is controlled by a self-locking lever. The dash board is completed with the usual instruments—starting magneto, main switch, petrol pressure gauges, oil pressure gauges, air pump, and petrol lever indicator. On the right-hand side of the pilot's seat is a lever controlling the clutch of the wireless dynamo drive.

LEVEL INDICATOR.

A level indicator of the type shown in Figure 29 is fitted on the dash board. It is of a type not previously found on German aeroplanes. It consists of a pendulum device, operating a circular disc, the lower half of which is covered by a semi-circular metal shield. The upper half of the disc is dark in colour, though not quite so dark as the shield, and below its horizontal diameter the swinging disc is painted white so that if the machine side slips a white sector becomes visible against a dark background as indicated in the sketch. This instrument appears to be very much better made than the usual indicators fitted to German machines.

FIG. 30.

FIG. 31.

GUN MOUNTING

A notable feature of the Halberstadt machine, is the fitting of the gun ring which is not incorporated in the fuselage, but is attached to its top surface by streamline steel struts. In front, it is supported by two converging steel tubes in a form of a " V " which branch from the upper fuselage longerons. The gun ring is thus very rigidly supported. Since the greater part of it is directly in the slip stream of the screw, it is made of very fair streamline section as may be gathered from the photograph No. A, and in general is much lighter and far better constructed than the usual German gun mounting. The accepted type of bracket and locking device is employed. Both portions of the ring are made of wood covered with doped fabric.

FABRIC.

The fabric is of the usual quality found on the better class of German aeroplanes. It is dyed with the familiar polygonal camouflaged scheme of colours and is applied to the wings with the warp and weft at an angle of 45 degrees to the spars. The reason for this method of wing covering is not clear. The dope used appears to be good. The body work and also the centre section of the top plane are covered with a scumble of colours arranged in indefinite areas and shading into one another. The colours used are a cloudy yellow, dark and light greens, brown, purple and a light blue. The belly of the fuselage is coloured yellow throughout.

FITTINGS.

In the floor of the observer's cockpit, is a bracket for a camera of one metre or more focal length. Detachable tubes for supporting the upper end of the camera are furnished and for this purpose clips are fitted on the fuselage members. A sliding trap door underneath the camera fitting is provided. Plugs at convenient points are arranged for the electrical heating circuit. The observer's seat is of the folding type, and is placed very low so that when he occupies it, the observer is well below the level of the top of the fuselage, and is thus completely hidden from view. The pilot's seat is adjustable fore and aft and is carried on light built up cross bars dropped into sockets bolted to the fuselage members. The form of the sockets is shown in Figure 31.

COMPASS.

The compass, which is of the usual German pattern, presenting no new features, is fitted in a circular box near the root of the left hand wing, where it is immediately under the view of the pilot.

SCHEDULE OF PRINCIPAL WEIGHTS.

	2532 lbs.
Total weight	lbs. ozs.
Upper wing, complete with aileron, aileron rod, drag bracing, and strut attachments, but without lift bracing wires and fabric	62 6
Lower wing, as above (no aileron fitted)	52 8
Aileron complete, without fabric	7 12
Aileron bar, with flange	4 0
Interplane strut, front, without bolts	3 3
,, ,, rear, ,, ,, ...	3 14
Centre section, complete, with radiator and gravity tank, aileron control crank, and bracing wires	101 0
Fixed tail plane (each), with fabric	7 8
Rudder, complete, with fabric	7 8
Elevator, complete, with hinge clips and fabric	12 0
Fin, complete, with fabric	9 . 6
V centre section strut	2 7
Straight centre section strut	3 2½
Undercarriage, complete, with struts and bracing, wheels, tyres, and shock absorbers ...	102 0
Shock absorber (multiple coil spring type), each	4 6
Axle, with shock absorber bobbins and caps	14 8
Wheel, with tyre	20 4
Tyre and tube	8 12
Wings, leading spar, per foot run	1 4
Wings, trailing spar, per foot run	0 14½

HISTORICAL NOTE.

The present Halberstadt fighter is a development of the earlier single-seater, an example of which was brought down on 29.10.17. In the latter case ash was used to a fairly large extent, both in the fuselage and wings, but in the more modern design spruce is exclusively adopted. The rear spar was of the ordinary I Section type without three-ply reinforcement. The fuselage, of somewhat similar shape, was fabric covered. Balanced elevators and rudder were fitted, but no fixed tail-plane or fin. The arrangement of the centre section, with tank and radiator, was substantially the same. Double bags of interplane struts were adopted, but the struts themselves were of the welded-up tapered pattern. The ailerons were controlled by wires and not, as in the present example, positively. Both planes had the same chord and the upper wings had an overhang. The weight of the complete machine, without pilot, was 1778 lbs.

Both the Halberstadt machines are at the Enemy Aircraft View Room, Agricultural Hall, Islington, where they may be seen on production of a pass, obtainable from the Controller, Technical Dept., Ap. D. (L.), Pen Corner House, Kingsway, W.C.2.

W. G. A.
Ap.D. (L.)

J. G. WEIR,
Brig.-General,
Controller, Technical Dept.

A.—View of Underside of Centre Section, Showing Radiator and Shutter, Machine Gun, and Cabane Struts.

B.—View of Cockpits, Showing Aileron Cranks, Gun Ring, Radiator, and Gravity Petrol Tank.

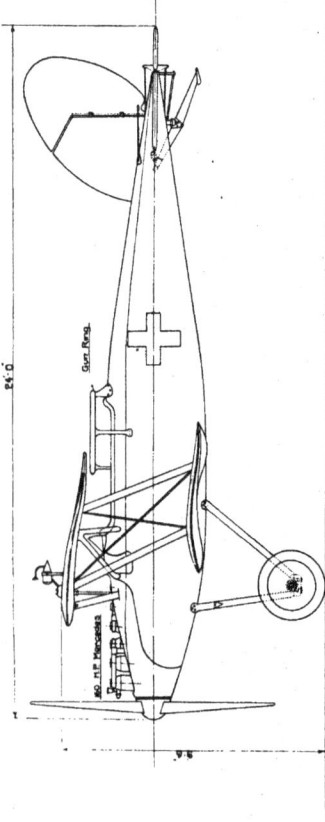

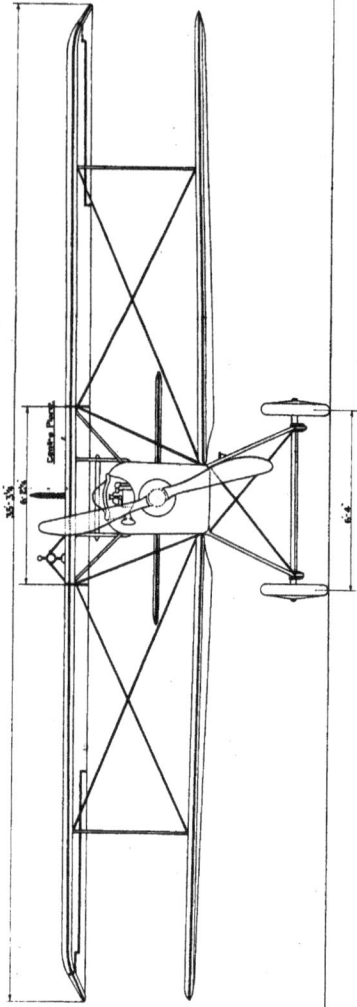

HALBERSTADT

Scale ½ = 1 Foot

GENERAL DETAILS.

TWO SEATER BIPLANE.

SPAN - 35'-3¼".   HEIGHT - 9'-6".

GAP 4'-0" TO 3'-8½".   ENGINE - 160 H.P.

CHORD TOP PLANE 5'-3¼".   SET BACK OF PLANES - 4".

CHORD BOTTOM PLANE - 4'-3½".   PROPELLER - 9'-0".

OVERALL LENGTH - 24'-0".   TRACK - 6'-4".

TAIL PLANE SPAN - 8'-11".   STAGGER - 2'-0".

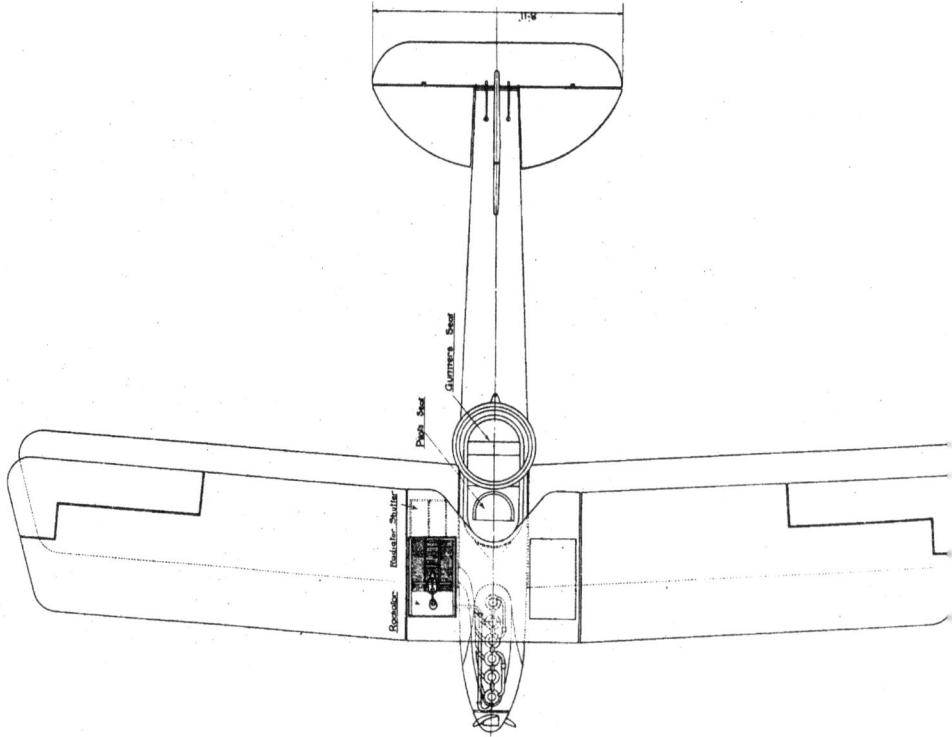

44255

MINISTRY OF MUNITIONS.

Technical Department - Aircraft Production.

I.C. 652.

Kingsway,

W.C. 2.

HALBERSTADT, C.L. IV. TYPE.

REPORT

ON THE

HALBERSTADT FIGHTER

TYPE C.L. IV.

OCTOBER, 1918.

J. G. WEIR,

Brigadier-General,

Controller, Technical Department.

REPORT

ON THE

Halberstadt Two-Seater, Type C.L. IV.

This machine, which is allotted G/5Bd:./22, landed near Chipilly on August 23, 1918. Dates stamped on the main planes give the date of construction as July, 1918.

It is very similar in design and construction to the C.L.II. type, which has already been fully reported upon (I.C.642), but many detail differences are incorporated.

Below is a comparative list of the principal dimensions of both C.L.II. and C.L.IV. types.

	C.L.IV.	C.L.II.
Span of upper plane	35ft. 2¼in.	35ft. 3¼in.
Span of lower plane	34ft. 9¼in.	34ft. 11in.
Chord of upper plane...	5ft. 2⅝in.	5ft. 3¼in.
Chord of lower plane	4ft. 3½in.	4ft. 3½in.
Gap, maximum	4ft. 4in.	4ft. 0in.
Gap, minimum	4ft. 0in.	3ft. 8½in.
Dihedral angle of lower plane	2 deg.	2 deg.
Horizontal dihedral of main planes	4 deg.	4 deg.
Total area of main planes	308 sq. ft.	310 sq. ft.
Area of each aileron	12 sq. ft.	12 sq. ft.
Area of aileron balance	2.0 sq. ft	2.0 sq. ft.
Area of tail planes	16 sq. ft.	13.6 sq. ft.
Area of elevator	13.6 sq. ft.	12.4 sq. ft.
Area of fin	11.4 sq. ft.	6.4 sq. ft.
Area of rudder	7.9 sq. ft.	7.9 sq. ft.
Area of rudder balance	1.0 sq. ft.	1.0 sq. ft.
Horizontal area of body	36 sq. ft.	44 sq. ft.
Vertical area of body	41 sq. ft.	52.8 sq ft
Length overall	20ft. 11½in.	24ft. 0in.
Engine	180 Merc.	180 Merc.
Capacity of petrol tanks	34 galls.	34 galls.
Capacity of oil system	4 galls.	4 galls.
Crew	Two	Two
Guns	One fixed and one movable.	

WINGS.

The wings, both in disposition and construction, are substantially the same as in the former machine. The characteristic wash-out at the root of the lower planes is even more pronounced than was the case in the C.L.II. machine. It will be seen from photograph A that the rear spar is bent and twisted by this wash-out. The exact shape of the trailing edge of one of the lower planes is shown in the scale drawings.

Fig. 1 gives a section of the upper wing drawn to scale, and Fig. 2 a comparison of the upper aerofoil of the C.L.IV. with the R.A.F.14 section, which is dotted. From Fig. 1 it will be noticed that the three-ply surrounds to the spars are still employed. They are drawn to scale in Fig. 3.

The ailerons remain unaltered in the C.L.IV. machine, and this is also true of the interplane and centre section struts.

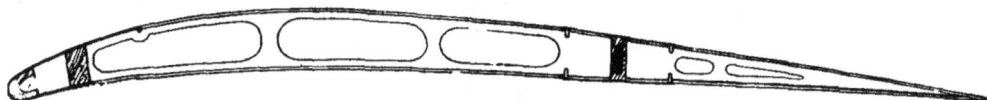

Fig. 1.

Fig. 2.

The attachment of upper wings to centre section and of lower wings to fuselage are unaltered, except that the tube which, in the earlier machine, passed right across the fuselage and connected the spars of the port and starboard lower wings is no longer found. Its place is taken by two fuselage fittings of the type shown in Fig. 4.

FUSELAGE.

Although the fuselage of the C.L.IV. machine is very like that of the C.L.II. type, the machine now being described has a body which is practically 3 feet shorter than that of the earlier machine.

Photograph A.

This shows the internal construction of a lower plane. Notice the pronounced wash-out.

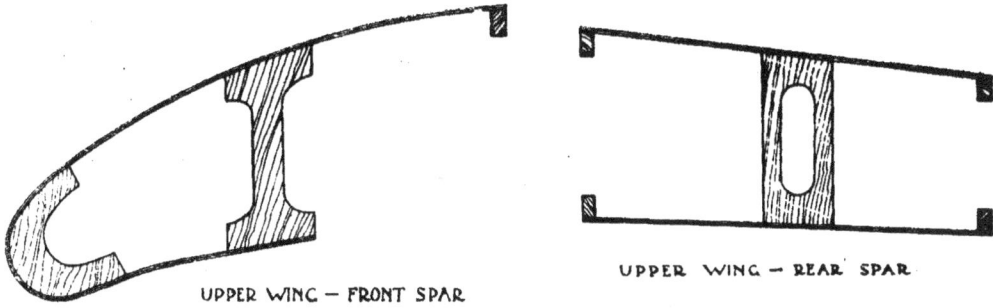

UPPER WING — FRONT SPAR

UPPER WING — REAR SPAR

Fig. 3.

TAIL PLANES AND SKID.

It is in these components that the greatest differences between the two types are found. The tail plane is now in one piece, and is laid across the rear of the fuselage, and attached there by the bolts shown in Fig. 6. The undivided elevator is now balanced, and the aspect ratio of the whole horizontal tail is larger than was the case in the earlier model. Besides this the actual area is greater. (It has been remarked that the C.L.IV. body is 3 feet shorter.)

The fin and rudder were not salved, and comparison is therefore not possible, but it is clear from the fuselage design that the fin is a separate unit simply attached to the body,

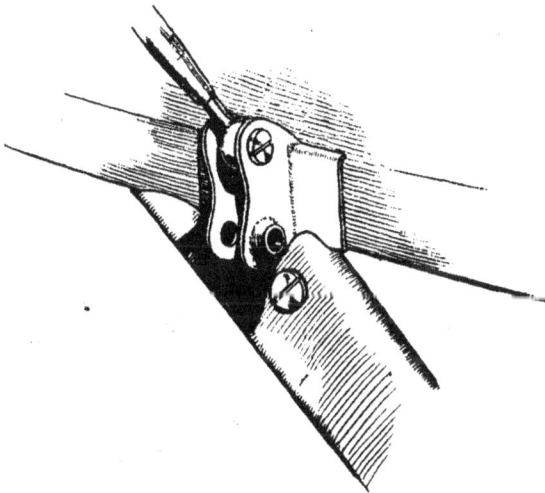

Fig. 4.

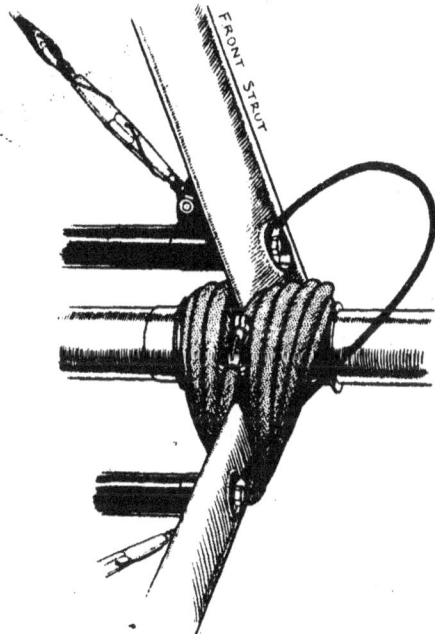

Fig. 5.

and not an integral part of it. It is also established that the rudder post is now found in the same vertical plane as the leading edge of the elevator. It will be remembered that the rudder post, in the C.L.II. type, was fixed more than a foot forward of the elevator fulcrum.

The inverted camber of the C.L.II. tail plane is now abolished, and a symmetrical camber substituted, and the rather elaborate tail skid of the earlier model has been simplified to the type found in the modern L.V.G. biplanes. In this type the skid is entirely exposed, and is pivoted on the lower edge of a small triangular fin under the tail plane. (See photograph and general arrangement drawings.)

UNDERCARRIAGE.

The landing gear is substantially the same as in the C.L.II. machine, but, as may be seen in Fig. 5, two compression tubes now run parallel to the axle, instead of one, as before.

FITTINGS.

The gun ring has been additionally stayed in front, but otherwise remains the same. It was fitted with a Parabellum gun.

Two fixed guns of the Spandau type are arranged for, one each side of the camshaft, but only the one on the starboard side was fitted at the time of capture.

A ten-loop Very cartridge belt is tacked to the top of the fuselage just behind the cockpit—it may be seen in the photograph—and a total of twelve light hand grenades may be carried in the wooden racks, one of which may be seen on either side of the fuselage.

The practice of enclosing the control wires in the cockpit is still continued, but aluminium shields are used instead of the more permanent three-ply construction.

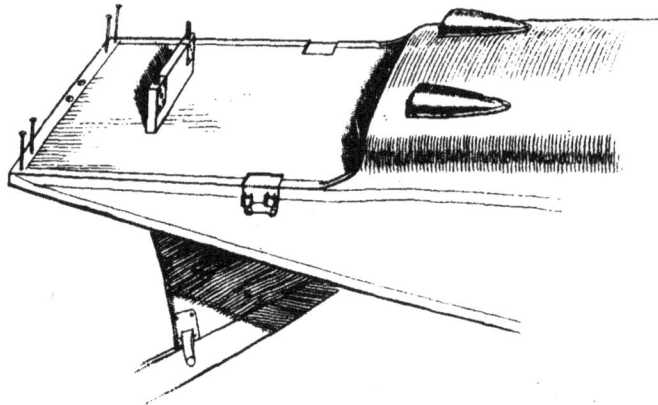

Fig. 6.

The machine is internally wired, but no wireless apparatus was on board at the time of capture. The dynamo bracket is no longer to be found alongside the engine, but is now on the front port undercarriage strut, and is driven by a propeller.

The pilot's seat is a shallow three-ply bucket, which rests on two cross pieces of wood supported on ribbed brass strips sweated to the top of the petrol tank, thus providing a fair amount of adjustment. This is the subject of a sketch (Fig. 7).

The fabric is throughout of the usual colour-printed type.

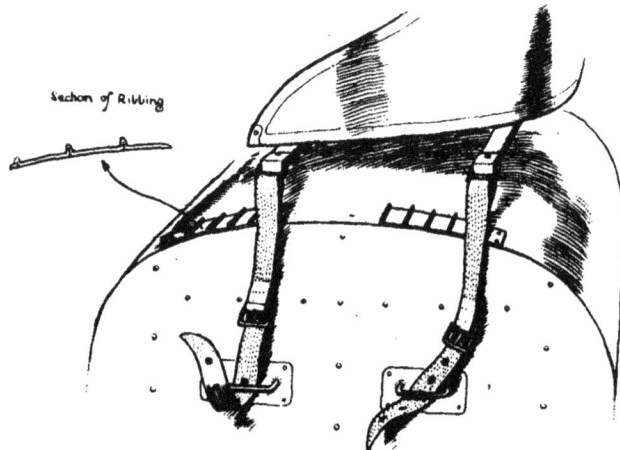

Section of Ribbing

Fig. 7.

SCHEDULE OF WEIGHTS, HALBERSTADT, C.L.IV.

	lbs.	ozs.
Body, with undercarriage, engine, Spandau gun, petrol tank, gauges, and controls	1220	0
Engine (dry), 180 Mercedes	635	0
Upper wing, complete (no bracing wires)	70	8
Lower wing, complete (with bracing wires)	64	0
Centre section, complete with struts and wiring) ...	108	8
Gravity petrol tank	11	4
Radiator	36	0
Centre section strut (Vee)	5	3
Centre section strut (straight	2	4
Interplane strut (front), with cable...	4	8
Interplane strut (rear), with cable...	4	0
Undercarriage, complete, approximately	112	0
Shock absorber (one)	4	6
Axle, with bobbins and caps	14	8
Wheel, complete with tyre	20	4
Tyre and tube	8	12
Leading spar of wings (per foot run)	1	4
Trailing spar of wings (per foot run)		14½
Tail plane and elevator (covered)	25	0

The aeroplane is in the Enemy Aircraft View Rooms, Islington, and may be seen on production of a pass, to be obtained by writing to:—The Controller, Technical Department, Ap.D. (L), Central House, Kingsway, W.C. 2.

W. G. A. Ap.D (L).

J. G. WEIR,
Brigadier-General,
Controller, Technical Department.

6

Photograph B.
Side View of Dismantled Halberstadt.

Photograph C.
Rear View of Fuselage and Tail of C.L.IV. Halberstadt.

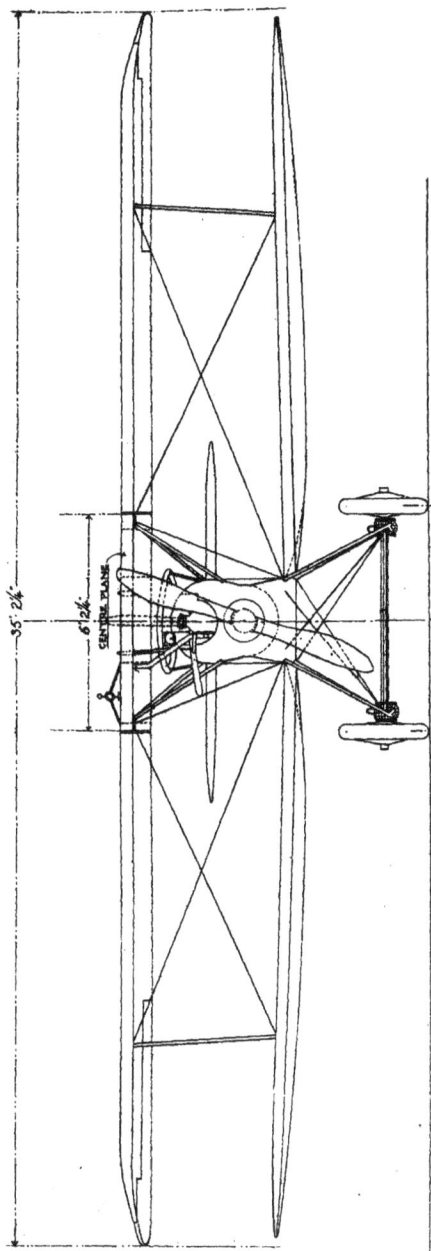

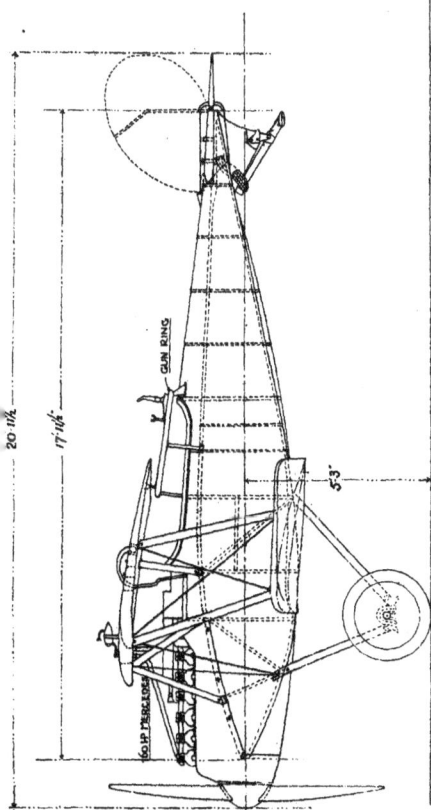

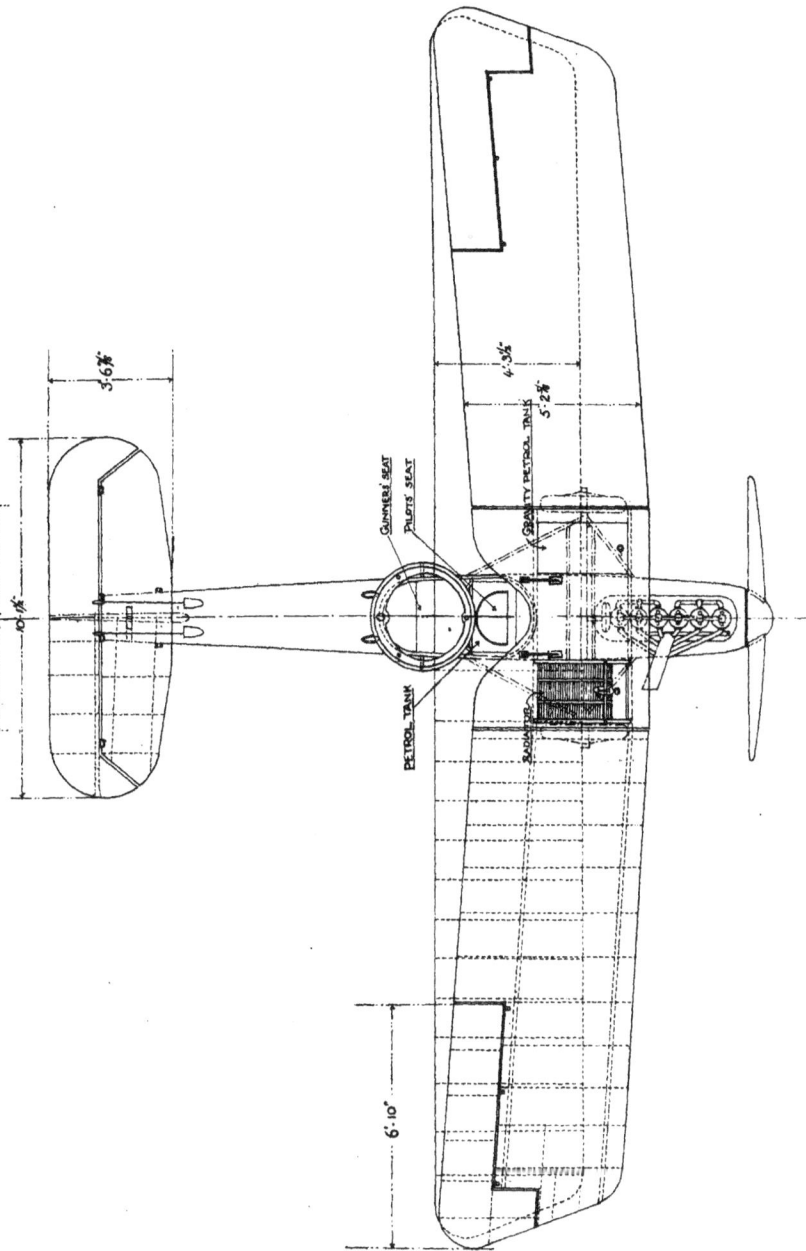

HALBERSTADT C4

SCALE.

INCHES ┃ FEET

GENERAL DETAILS.

SPAN UPPER PLANE   35'-2¼'
SPAN LOWER PLANE   34'-9¾'
CHORD UPPER PLANE   5'-2⅝'
CHORD LOWER PLANE   4'-3½'
LENGTH OVERALL   20'-11½'
SPAN TAIL PLANE   10'-1½'
GAP   4'-4" TO 4'-0"
SET BACK OF TOP PLANE -4°
STAGGER   2'-0" TO 1'-2"

CENTRE PLANE

GUNNER'S SEAT
PILOT'S SEAT
GRAVITY PETROL TANK
PETROL TANK

GUN RING
160 H.P. MERCEDES

D.C.Q.E. T.5 R.7359 1100 10/18

www.ingramcontent.com/pod-product-compliance
Lightning Source LLC
Chambersburg PA
CBHW081543090426
42741CB00014BA/3249